THIS BOOK BELONGS TO

Brooks

# for Alexander

Copyright © 1988 by Charlotte Voake

First American edition

Library of Congress Cataloging-in-Publication Data

Voake, Charlotte.
  First things first  /  Charlotte Voake. — 1st ed.
    p.   cm.
  Summary: An illustrated introduction for babies to numbers, the alphabet,
shapes, colors, days of the week, seasons, birds, insects, rhymes, and lullabies.
ISBN 0-316-90510-0
  [1. Picture books.]   I. Title.
  PZ7.V855Fi   1988
[E] — dc19
                                          87-37536
                                             CIP
                                             AC

10  9  8  7  6  5  4  3  2  1

Printed and bound by L.E.G.O., Vicenza, Italy

# FIRST Things FIRST

## CHARLOTTE VOAKE

*Joy Street Books*
Little, Brown and Company
Boston · Toronto

Sit, crawl, stand ............................................ 8 and 9

THE ALPHABET ............................ 10 and 11
and Great A, Little a ... a b c ............ 12

Tommy Snooks and Bessy Brooks ............ 13
and DAYS of the WEEK ............ 14 and 15

One, two, three, four, five, Once I caught
a fish alive ............ 16
and SOME FISHES ............ 17

NUMBERS ............ 18 and 19
One Cat ............ 20
One Dog ............ 21

# TENTS

SOME ANIMALS .......... 22 and 23

Two Cows .......... 24 and 25

COLORED RIBBONS .......... 26 and 27

Cars and Boats and Planes .......... 28 and 29

THREE SHAPES .......... 30

and Round About, round about, Gooseberry pie .......... 31

SOME FRUIT .......... 32 and 33

and LOTS OF INSECTS .......... 34 and 35

A CAULIFLOWER, and SOME PEAS ... 36

Pease Porridge Hot .......... 37

Ring-a-ring o' roses .......... 38 and 39

and FLOWERS .......... 40 and 41

BIRDS .......... 42, 43, 44.

Zz

Sit

Crawl Stand

Walk  Run Jump

8

# Listen

# Shout

# Touch

# Look

# Smell

# Eat

a · b · c · d · e · f · g · h · i · j · k · l · m · n

a b c d e f

n o p q r s t

10 A · B · C · D · E · F · G · H · I · J · K · L · M

o · p · q · r · s · t · u · v · w · x · y · z

g h i j k l m

u v w x y z

12

AS Tommy Snooks
And Bessy Brooks
Went walking out
On Sunday,
Said Tommy Snooks
To Bessy Brooks,
"Tomorrow will be Monday!"

Monday's child is fair of face

MONDAY

Tuesday's child is full of grace

TUESDAY

Saturday's child works hard for a living

SATURDAY

Friday's child is loving and giving

FRIDAY

14

WEDNESDAY

THURSDAY

SUNDAY

ONE, Two, three, four, five,
Once I caught a fish alive,

Six, seven, eight, nine, ten,
Then I let it go again.

Why did you let it go?
Because it bit my finger so.
Which finger did it bite?
This little finger on the right.

A LONG, THIN, WIGGLY FISH

A STRIPY FISH

A FLAT, GREEN, SPOTTY FISH!

17

# ONE CAT

HERE Am I, little Jumping Joan,
When nobody's with me,
I'm always alone.

# ONE DOG

BOW Wow wow
Whose dog art thou?
Little Tom Tinker's dog,
Bow wow wow

Squirrel SOME
LION
Mouse Rat
Panda POLAR BEAR Kangaroos

# ANIMALS

TIGER

Rabbits

Horse

CAMEL

Elephant

23

## TWO

THE Friendly cow all red and white
  I love with all my heart;
She gives me cream with all her might,
  To eat with apple tart.

24

Robert Louis Stevenson

# COWS

I Never saw a purple cow,
I never hope to see one;
But I can tell you anyhow,
I'd rather see than be one!

Gelett Burgess

25

# COLORED

PURPLE

RED

# RIBBONS

BLUE  YELLOW  BROWN  PINK  ORANGE  GREEN  Black

Red truck

Gray plane

Brown
trailer

Green tractor

28

Pink car

Blue train

Yellow boat

Black bike

29

# THREE SHAPES

triangle

square

circle

ROUND About, round about,
   Gooseberry pie,
My father loves pie,
   And so do I!

SOME FRUIT

Tinker
Tailor
Soldier
Sailor
Rich Man

CHERRIES

Thief
Beggar Man
Poor Man

Strawberry

Banana

PEAR

APPLE

and...

33

Lacewing

Housefly

LOTS OF

Grasshopper

Crane Fly

Moths

Bee

Ladybug

Earwig

Ants

34

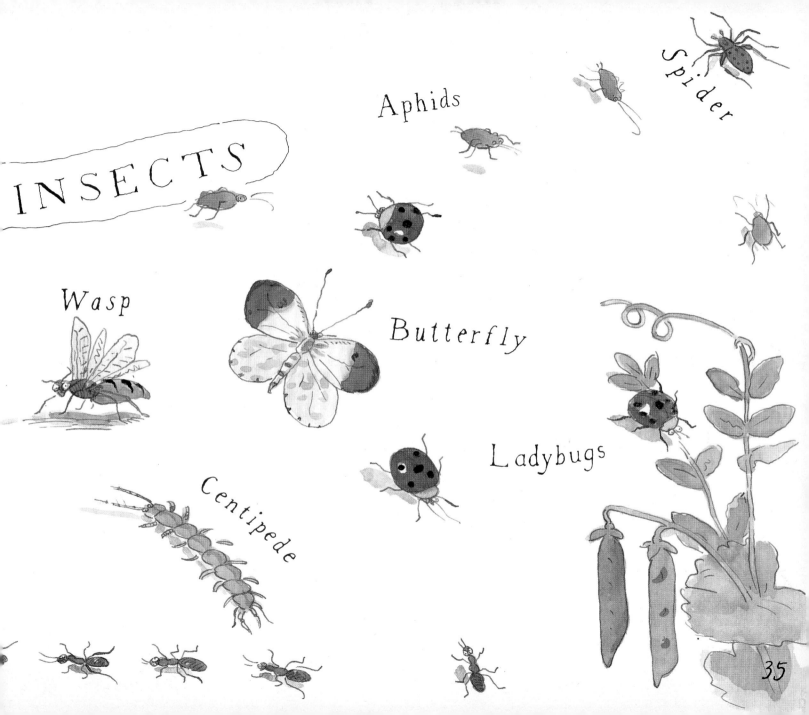

INSECTS

Aphids

Spider

Wasp

Butterfly

Ladybugs

Centipede

35

# A GREAT BIG

CAULIFLOWER

And some LITTLE TINY Peas.

PEASE Porridge hot,
Pease porridge cold,
Pease porridge in the pot,
Nine days old!

37

Ring-a-ring o'roses,
A Pocket full of posies,

38

Violet

F L O W

Dandelion

Daffodil

ERS

Buttercup

Shepherd's Purse

Daisy

41

# A DUCK  and

TWO MAGPIES  A Robin

A GOOSE

A Hen

A Blackbird

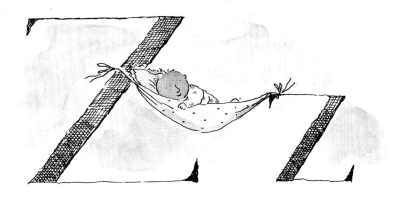

TU-Whit, tu-whoo,
Goodnight to you!